T0081717

FELIX MENDELSSOHN-BARTHOLDY

CONCERTO

for

VIOLIN

and

ORCHESTRA

E MINOR ✦ E MOLL

OPUS 64

To access audio visit:
www.halleonard.com/mylibrary

Enter Code
1347-0005-6786-4443

ISBN 978-1-59615-098-0

MMO Music Minus One

EXCLUSIVELY DISTRIBUTED BY

Hal•Leonard®

7777 W. BLUEMOUND RD. P.O. BOX 13819 MILWAUKEE, WI 53213

© 2003 MMO Music Group, Inc.
All Rights Reserved

For all works contained herein:
Unauthorized copying, arranging, adapting, recording, Internet posting, public performance,
or other distribution of the printed or recorded music in this publication is an infringement of copyright.
Infringers are liable under the law.

Visit Hal Leonard Online at
www.halleonard.com

Music Minus One

3101

CONTENTS

CONCERTO

for

VIOLIN and ORCHESTRA

E MINOR · E MOLL

op. 64

Felix Mendelssohn-Bartholdy
(1809-1847)

Solo Violin

Allegro molto appassionato

4

6

MMO 3101

II.

III.

*The original score here gives a fingering of 3, which must be an engraver's error.

Engraving: Wieslaw Novak